Brother, I Want to Know Your Story

This book is for

_____

Brother, I Want to Know Your Story © 2021 MadGaviette Publishing
All rights reserved. No part of this book may be used or reproduced in any manner whatsoever without written permissions

Introduction

The purpose of this book to share more of yourself with your beloved brothers and sisters. By sharing your life story, thoughts and memories, they will be able to know you in an entirely new way. They'll discover the important details and moments that formed the foundation of your life, and also the little things that helped you to become the person they know and love today.

This book will become a cherished family heirloom that will be passed down to future generations to teach them about their family's history, roots and values.

The book is divided into sections, beginning with your early childhood memories and details. Each section features writing prompts for you to answer, followed by several pages for you to record other memories, thoughts and life lessons learned that you would like to share. Take your time in filling out the answers: there are no right or wrong responses.

The gift of your story and accumulated wisdom is one that your family will cherish in the years to come!

Table of Contents

Introduction 2

Roots: My Family Tree 4

In the beginning:
    Childhood Memories 5

Growing up: Adolescence 17

On my own: Young Adulthood 27

Starting a family: Marriage & Children 38

Working years: Earning a Living 51

Time goes on: Getting Older 61

More about me:
    My Values & Beliefs 73
    My Interests & Favorites 77

Roots:
My Family Tree

My Grandfather

My Grandfather

My Grandmother

My Grandmother

My Mother

My Father

Me

In the beginning: Childhood Memories

In the beginning:
Childhood Memories

What is your full name?

___

Were you named after someone, or does your name have any special meaning or significance?

___

What was your date of birth and where were you born?

___

How old were your parents when you were born?

___

Do you know what size you were at birth?

___

Did you have any nicknames?

___

How many siblings did you have? Were they older or younger than you? What are their names?

_____
_____
_____
_____

Did your parents share any special stories about you as a baby or very young child?

_____
_____
_____
_____
_____
_____
_____
_____
_____
_____
_____
_____
_____
_____
_____
_____
_____
_____

What is your earliest memory?

_____
_____
_____
_____

Did you have any serious childhood accidents or illnesses?

_____
_____
_____

What were your parents' names, when were they born and where did they grow up?

_____
_____
_____

Describe any special memories of your mother and what she was like when you were little.

_____
_____
_____
_____
_____
_____
_____

Describe any special memories of your father and what he was like when you were little.

_____
_____
_____
_____
_____
_____
_____
_____
_____
_____
_____
_____

Describe any special memories of your grandparents or other close family members when you were little.

_____
_____
_____
_____
_____
_____
_____
_____
_____
_____
_____
_____
_____
_____

What was your favorite holiday growing up?
_____
_____

Were there any family traditions that made it special?
_____
_____
_____
_____

Did you have birthday parties? What were they like?
_____
_____
_____
_____
_____

What family vacations stand out in your memory?
_____
_____
_____
_____
_____
_____
_____
_____
_____

What did you want to be when you grew up?

_____
_____

What were your childhood home and neighborhood like?

_____
_____
_____
_____

Were you afraid of anything as a child, such as the dark or spiders?

_____
_____
_____

Did you believe in Santa Claus, the Easter Bunny, the Tooth Fairy, etc? What were your family traditions?

_____
_____
_____
_____
_____
_____
_____
_____

Childhood Memories

Childhood Memories

Childhood Memories

Childhood Memories

Childhood Memories

Growing up:
Adolescence

Growing up:
Adolescence

What schools did you attend growing up? Where were they?

_____
_____
_____
_____

Did you like school? What were your favorite and least favorite subjects?

_____
_____
_____
_____

What school clubs and activities were you involved in?

_____
_____
_____
_____
_____
_____
_____
_____

What activities were you involved in outside of school?
___
___
___
___

Did you participate in any sports?
___
___
___
___

Did you learn to play a musical instrument?
___
___

How were your grades?
___
___

Do you have any special memories of attending Prom, Homecoming, etc.?
___
___
___
___
___

Who were your friends and what did you like to do together?

_____
_____
_____
_____

How old were you when you learned to drive and who taught you? Did you have a car?

_____
_____
_____

Were you allowed to date? At what age? Who was your first date with and what did you do?

_____
_____
_____
_____
_____

What type of clothing did you like to wear in high school? Was your hair long or short?

_____
_____
_____
_____
_____
_____

What type of music did you listen to and who were your favorite artists? Favorite song?

_____
_____
_____
_____

How was your relationship with your parents during those years?

_____
_____
_____
_____

Did you go on any special trips with your family or school?

_____
_____
_____

Did you have a graduation celebration?

_____
_____
_____
_____
_____
_____

Adolescent Memories

Adolescent Memories

Adolescent Memories

Adolescent Memories

Adolescent Memories

On my own:
Young Adulthood

On my own:
Young Adulthood

Did you attend school after high school? If not, why not?

_____
_____
_____

If so, where did your attend college and what did you major in? Did you graduate?

_____
_____
_____

Where did you live while in college?

_____
_____
_____

Which of the things you learned in school has been the most helpful to you in the real world?

_____
_____
_____
_____

What organized activities were you involved in during college?

___

How did you and your friends spend your spare time?

___

Did you study abroad? If so, where and what did you like the most about the experience?

___

How long did it take to find your first job after graduating? What was it?

___

Did you serve in the military? If so, for how long? Which branch? What rank did you achieve and what was your job?

_____
_____
_____
_____
_____
_____

Where were you stationed or deployed?

_____
_____
_____

Did you see combat?

_____
_____

How did your military service change you?

_____
_____
_____
_____
_____
_____
_____
_____

Where did you live after leaving home and who did you live with?

_____
_____
_____

Have you ever experienced "love at first sight" and did it work out?

_____
_____
_____
_____

What was the most romantic date you remember ever going on?

_____
_____
_____
_____
_____

What was the worst date you remember?

_____
_____
_____
_____
_____

Young Adult Memories

Young Adult Memories

Young Adult Memories

Young Adult Memories

Young Adult Memories

Starting a family:
Marriage & Children

Starting a family:
Marriage & Children

How did you meet your wife?

What qualities attracted you to her?

What did you do on your first date together?

How long did you date before you got engaged? How long were you engaged before you got married?

___

___

___

How did you propose?

___

___

___

___

When and where did you get married?

___

___

What do you remember most about your wedding?

___

___

___

___

___

Did you go on a honeymoon? Where did you go?

___

___

___

Where was your first home together and what was it like?
___
___
___
___
___
___
___

Where did you each work?
___
___
___
___

What did you do for fun as a couple in the early years?
___
___
___
___
___

What was the hardest thing to adjust to about being married?
___
___
___
___
___

How did you divide the household chores?
___
___
___

How did you celebrate your first anniversary?
___
___
___
___

Did you take any special trips together?
___
___
___
___

What do you love most about your wife?
___
___
___

What does she do that drives you crazy?
___
___
___

How long were you married before your first child arrived?

How did it feel, knowing that you were about to become a father?

What are your children's names and birthdates?

How did becoming a father change your life?

Did you get to watch your children being born?

Did you raise your children in the same way that your parents raised you, or did you do things differently?

How old were you when I was born?

What special memories do you have of me as a child?

What do you love best about me?

_____
_____
_____
_____

What makes you proudest as a brother?

_____
_____
_____
_____
_____

What are your favorite traditions within our family?

_____
_____
_____
_____
_____

What was your favorite family trip while your children were growing up?

_____
_____
_____
_____
_____
_____

What are some special family times that you remember of us?

Is there anything you wish you had done differently as a brother?

Family Memories

Family Memories

Family Memories

Family Memories

Family Memories

The working years: Earning a Living

The working years:
Earning a Living

What was your first job?

_____
_____
_____
_____

What jobs have you held during your life?

_____
_____
_____
_____
_____
_____
_____
_____

What is your profession?

_____
_____
_____
_____
_____
_____
_____
_____

How did you learn to do your job?

What is the best job you ever had? What did you most like about it?

What was your least favorite job? Why?

Which job was the most fun?

Did your career turn out as you expected?

Is there a job you would like to have held, but never had the opportunity?

Who was your favorite boss and why?

What did you dislike the most about having to go to work each day?

_____
_____
_____
_____

Did your work give you a sense of fulfillment?

_____
_____
_____
_____
_____
_____
_____
_____
_____

What are you looking forward to in retirement?

_____
_____
_____
_____
_____
_____
_____
_____
_____

Work Memories

Work Memories

Work Memories

Work Memories

Work Memories

Time goes on: Getting Older

Time goes on:
Getting Older

What places are still on your bucket list to visit?

_____
_____
_____
_____
_____
_____

What things are on your bucket list yet to try doing?

_____
_____
_____
_____
_____
_____

How have your priorities changed as you've gotten older?

_____
_____
_____
_____
_____
_____
_____
_____
_____

Do you have any health challenges?

_____
_____
_____
_____
_____

Of what accomplishment are you most proud so far?

_____
_____
_____
_____
_____
_____
_____
_____
_____

Is there anything you would change about your life if you could?

_____
_____
_____
_____
_____
_____
_____

What are you most thankful for in your life?

_____
_____
_____
_____
_____

If you could say anything to your younger self, what would it be?

_____
_____
_____
_____
_____

Is there anything you wish you had known sooner?

_____
_____
_____
_____
_____

Who has had the biggest influence on your life?

_____
_____
_____
_____
_____

If you could revisit any period in your life, when would it be and why?

_____
_____
_____
_____
_____
_____
_____

What events in your life do you feel helped make you who you are today?

_____
_____
_____
_____
_____
_____
_____

What would you like your legacy to be?

_____
_____
_____
_____
_____
_____
_____

How many grandchildren do you have? What are their names and when were they born?

How did your life change when you became a grandparent?

How are you different with your grandchildren than you were with your own children?

What do you love the most about being a grandparent?

What hopes do you have for your grandchildren?

Do you have any great-grandchildren? What are their names and when were they born?

Later Memories

Later Memories

Later Memories

Later Memories

Later Memories

More about me:
My Values & Beliefs

More about me:
My Values & Beliefs

Do you believe in God?

_____
_____
_____
_____
_____

Do you pray, and if so, how often?

_____
_____
_____
_____

Are you a member of an organized religion? If so, which one?

_____
_____
_____
_____

Do you attend regular religious services or meetings?

_____
_____
_____

Do you belong to a political party? Which one?
_____
_____

Do you vote?
_____
_____

Have you ever been the victim of prejudice for any reason?
_____
_____
_____
_____
_____
_____
_____

What do you think can be done to overcome prejudice?
_____
_____
_____
_____

Were you taught any personal prejudices as a child?
_____
_____
_____

What values do you feel are most important?

Have you been able to incorporate these values into your family?

What changes would you like to see in the world to make it a better place?

More about me:
My Interests & Favorites

Do you have any hobbies? Why do you enjoy them?

_____
_____
_____
_____
_____

What other hobbies have you tried? Why did you stop doing them?

_____
_____
_____
_____
_____

Do you collect anything?

_____
_____
_____

What was your first car? What is your favorite car?

_____
_____

Do you enjoy traveling? Do you have a passport?

_____
_____

What countries have you visited and which was your favorite?

_____
_____
_____
_____
_____
_____
_____

What languages do you speak?

_____
_____
_____

How many states have you visited? Which do you like best?

_____
_____
_____
_____
_____
_____
_____

What is your favorite city to visit?

_____
_____

Would you rather fly or drive?
___

Where is your favorite vacation spot?
___

What is your favorite way to spend a weekend?
___
___
___
___

What is your favorite way to relax?
___
___
___
___

How would you describe your perfect day?
___
___
___
___
___
___
___

What sports have you played?
___
___

Which sports do you like to watch?
___
___
___

What are your favorite teams?
___
___
___

Do you play a musical instrument? If so, which one?
___

What is your favorite type of music to listen to?
___
___

Do you have a favorite song?
___

What was your favorite concert you've attended?
___
___

What do you do for exercise? Do you enjoy it?
_____
_____

Do you have a favorite museum?
_____

What is your favorite board game or card game?
_____
_____

What would you like to try doing, but haven't yet?
_____
_____
_____
_____

What genres do you enjoy reading?
_____
_____
_____

What is your favorite book? Who is your favorite author?
_____
_____

Do you prefer actual books, electronic books or audio books?
_____

Do you play video or any other electronic games?
_____
_____

What is your favorite TV show? What do you like about it?
_____
_____
_____

What is your favorite movie?
_____
_____

Have you ever been to a drive-in movie?
_____

Who are your favorite actor and actress?
_____
_____

Who would you most like to have a conversation with if you could, living or dead?
_____

What would you ask them?
_____
_____
_____

How do you like to spend your free time?

What do you think your talents are?

What do other people think you're good at?

What is your favorite animal?

What pets have you had during your lifetime?

If your parents have passed away, when did they die and what was the cause?

Are you a "morning person" or a "night owl?"
_____
_____

What are your favorite foods?
_____
_____
_____

What is your favorite restaurant and what do you like to order there?
_____
_____

What is your favorite dessert? Do you have a "sweet tooth?"
_____
_____

What are your favorite beverages -- hot, cold and cocktail?
_____
_____
_____

Do you have any superstitions?
_____
_____
_____
_____

Do you believe in astrology? What is your zodiac sign?
_____
_____

How many times have you been married?
_____
_____

What is your favorite color?
_____

What is your favorite day of the week?
_____

Do you like to gamble or buy lottery tickets?
_____
_____
_____

What is your favorite flower?
_____

Do you have a favorite type of weather? What is your favorite season?
_____
_____
_____
_____

Do you have a "lucky number?"

___

What kind of candy do you like best?

___

What is your favorite smell?

___

Do you have a favorite flower?

___

Do you enjoy cooking or baking? What is your specialty?

___
___
___

Do you have a favorite quote?

___
___
___
___

What is your favorite holiday?

___
___
___

Other Memories to Share

Other Memories to Share

Other Memories to Share

Other Memories to Share

Other Memories to Share

Other Memories to Share

Other Memories to Share

Other Memories to Share

Other Memories to Share

Other Memories to Share

Other Memories to Share

Other Memories to Share

Other Memories to Share

Final Thoughts

Made in United States
Cleveland, OH
11 January 2025